THE KEY TO OVERCOMING NEGATIVITIES THAT HINDER YOUR PRODUCTIVITY

Christy Obidigwe

Copyright © 2021 by Christy Obidigwe

FIRST EDITION

INTRODUCTION

Productivity is a word that describes what we give out. It could be knowledge, services rendered, skills expertise, etc.

In a world screaming for help in all its corners, begging for peace, rattled on all sides by chaos, terrorism, and wars, bedeviled by an unexplainable plague, and experiencing the worst batch of natural disasters cum economic landslides, a depressing effect has taken its toll on the productivity of hundreds of thousands all over the globe.

The recent scenarios have caused many to lose hope, the will to move on, or be optimistic about anything. Good fractions of mankind have become a shadow of themselves as they are defeated by the faceless menace of the difficult times that have presented themselves to humanity.

How can one overcome the challenges that prevent one from being productive? The answer lies within the lines below.

CHAPTER ONE

What are the negativities that often hinder productivity?

They include:

- Depression
- Corporate slavery
- Addiction to certain vices. Notorious on the list include masturbation, alcoholism, and pornography. Millions are bound by these vices.

How are they overcome? For each vice, we will:

- Take a brief tour of the vice.
- Look at its effects on individuals.
- Outline how it can be overcome.

CHAPTER TWO

A Brief Tour on What Depression is.

Depression is a state of mind wherein an individual feels sad or unhappy. This usually arises from a low self-worth perspective, an unpleasant, sad, or tragic incident that occurred in the life of such an individual. It means that whenever an individual feels depressed, he or she loses hope, and stops having a positive or encouraging outlook on life.

Depression does not begin overnight. It takes its hold over series of unpleasant experiences. These could be within or outside the scope of the following:

- The loss of a loved one.
- Consistent rejection.
- Consistent criticism.
- Failure to achieve a goal after several attempts.
- Temporal or long-term ill-health.
- Caring for a loved one who is ill.
- Low self-esteem.
- Taking care of sick people.
- A horrific experience.
- Financial dependence, lack, or instability.
- A sudden downgrade in your career.
- Low job satisfaction, or no job at all.
- An abusive relationship.
- Being discriminated against.
- Erratic interruptions to your job schedule such as prolonged protests, union strikes, etc.

The list goes on. These, as well a dozen other factors, form the basis for a catalog of unpleasant experiences.

These experiences are consistently exhumed or remembered by the individual *especially* when another unpleasant situation arises.

An individual can get sad over an incident. But when such sorrow lapses into a long-term duration extending for days, weeks, or months, it has slowly given way to depression.

Depression has claimed responsibility for:

- **Suicide:**
Thousands have lost their lives due to this. When a man loses the will to live on, the root of such a decision is deeply embedded in depression.

- **Mental instability:**
A deeper investigation into the root cause of the mental instabilities of affected individuals can be traced to depression.
- **Addiction:**
So many individuals, seeking a way of escape from reality, begin to take substances that help them lose consciousness for short periods. Others acquaint themselves with negative habits such as alcoholism etc.
  - Extreme and unhealthy anger, which drives the individual to inflict harm on others.
  - Lack of productivity.
  - Stagnation in key aspects of that individual's life.
  - Neglect of health, physical well-being, and in extreme cases, physical appearance.

The web of effects linked to depression is enormous. It looks harmless, but it is deadlier than the lethal feel of a poisoned dart. It poisons the mind, heart, emotions, well-being, and will of an individual. It has the capacity of crippling the entire setup of an individual's progress in life.

Sadly today, this menace has become an invited companion in the lives of many individuals. It has no respect for class, rank, or personality. It has no limits to its borders. It pervades every nation of the earth. It willingly takes its hold wherever it finds an opening, and like a leech, keeps asking for more, until the individual is consumed in its woes.

CHAPTER THREE

Having seen what depression is capable of. It is important to know how it can be tackled when it is encountered. Depression can be overcome with the following practical steps:

· Take a trip to the cemetery.
I can imagine the look of disgust on your face right now. But please do not be. Have a good look at the nearest tombstone. The individual lying beneath it no longer lives. You still have life in you. Life on its own is a *miracle.* It is something you have, but have no power over. It was given to you for a purpose.

The tombstone you may be looking at contains an individual who no longer exists. **You** still exist. You are alive. And **that** is something worth holding unto.

· Take   a   trip   to   the   nearest   hospital.

An outline of a health facility

You do not need to go in. You can stand at the entrance, and watch what is going on. You will see those who are alive, but can't walk, those in pain over their calamity, and can't do anything about it. What's worse, you may get to see an ambulance driving in, and the medical personnel bringing out a covered body or an individual who no longer moves. The destination is no longer the ward, but the morgue.

One day I felt low and hopeless. I tried to believe that remaining hopeless was the best way out of the situation until I visited the hospital. I went in. I had no sense of direction. The first line of thought was the postnatal ward, and I walked into it. At the far end was a young, quiet woman. Unlike other patients that had one or two companions around them, there was no one around her. I walked to her and greeted her. During our conversation, she told me that she had been stuck at the hospital for over a month. Puzzled, I asked her why, and she said that she had no one to pay her bills. I looked at the sleeping baby and asked her about the baby's father. She said sadly that he had absconded, and didn't show up even when told that the baby had arrived. I asked about her family, and she said that she had no nearby relative to fend for her. It took words out of my mouth. On my way out, I could hear the moans and wails of patients from different wards. I got home that day a changed person. Each time I felt sad, I reminded myself about that hospital. As at the time of the visitation, I had nothing except a few fruits I bought, which I gave to the young woman I had a conversation with. I had that lady in mind for a long time and wondered what became of her. But the visit left an indelible mark on me.

- **Make a conscious, deliberate effort to observe nature around you.**

When God's word asked us to look at the ant, it was not mincing words. Take a good look at the ant, a creature you can easily crush with the tip of your finger. But this tiny creature works tirelessly to gather what it eats. It has no car, no money, or luxury related to what we may have access to once in a while. But it gathers what it needs on a long-term basis.

Look at the clouds that float across the sky, right outside your window, just in case you don't have the means to go to the hospital or the cemetery. These clouds come in different shades.

A typical calm cloud

A boisterous cloud

There are days they come in peaceful, white, glowing, radiant, and beautiful shades. There are also days, they come as stormy, dark, gloomy, grey shades of clouds. On such days, they put out the sun, and prevent its warm glow on the earth. But it is not forever. Sooner or later, they give way, and the sun shines again.

What does this tell you? That there will be days filled with pleasant surprises, and there will be days that will be accompanied by various storms. It's not easy, and anyone who says it is lying. But therein lays that quiet determination expected of us as humans to have, just as God found with the ant. What is most important is that no matter how long it takes, the sun will shine again. It takes **our conscious decision** to drive away every gloomy thought, and see the sunshine in infallible truths.

The beauty of nature brings with it a soothing realization of the calm, peace, and rest we could all experience if we choose to do so.

• **Look inwards.**

Sometimes, we get all sad for the wrong reasons. Sometimes we get depressed over issues that may not be worth it. Look inwards. Ask yourself the following questions:

1) Why do I feel sad?
2) What can I do about it

It is one thing to know that you are sad. It is another to know **why** and to know **what to do about it**.

• **Talk to someone about your dilemma.**

Many suicides took place because there was no listening ear to hear, no shoulder to weep on, no hands to hold, and show comfort. So many individuals live daily, bearing the invisible weight of their sorrows, and pain upon their shoulders. They have no one to talk to and suffer in silence.

Sometimes, we do not need to look down on those who have pets and talk to them as though they are humans. What we do not realize is that if you don't get out what is plaguing you, it becomes corrosive to your system, and one way or another, it will explode someday. It could do so as suicide, murder, insanity, or an outright nervous breakdown.

There is a healing that comes when you release what is inside. And this is where prayer is very important for the Christian. When you have no reliable friend, colleague, or counselor to talk to, there is the invisible God who is **everywhere at the same time.** Right there in your room, you could talk to HIM. Let out all that is inside. Weep if you have to. It is okay to do so.

For those who do not have the disposition that Christians do, there **should be** good guidance and counseling personnel you could talk to. Ask friends, family, and colleagues for assistance in locating one. Any of these groups can help.

·Find out the purpose for which the particular cause of depression occurred in your life.

Sometimes, certain events take place in our life for a purpose. It was at the lowest points of my life that I usually received inspirations that have stayed with me till today.

Listen to your heart

Recently, I was watching a popular Christian TV show, and I listened to the story of a young woman who lost her brother, and mother (who was her grandmother) in one week. She had just returned from the burial of her brother and was getting ready to receive her grandma from the airport. She got to the airport only for her to be taken to the hospital to view the corpse. It was said that the grandma had collapsed on the plane. It was at that darkest moment that a hit song was sown in her heart.

Have you asked why you were allowed to pass through this peculiar situation? When you ask, it will be given to you.

· Get to hear the experiences of others.

There are TV shows that help bring to the limelight the experiences of others, and how they were able to overcome their challenges.

Learn to listen to what others have passed through.

Do your best to watch these shows or you can follow them on their social media handles. The experiences of others will help you overcome yours easily.

· Listen to inspirational music.

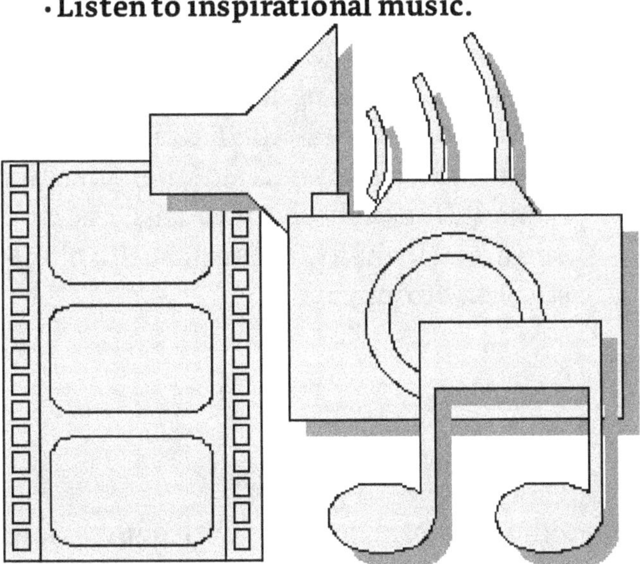

There are certain genres of music that help uplift your soul and calm soothing nerves.

Various mediums of music

There is a connection between what you hear and the state of your heart.

For the Christian, worship songs that expound on the greatness of God can be of great help. For those who do not share that disposition or don't have a flair for music, any of the above could be attempted.

· Finally, if you have tried all of the above, and nothing seems to be working out.

Permit me to say how sorry I am about your pain and discouragement. I know how it feels like, I have been there. If all of the above didn't work for you, this option won't. ***Keep holding on to the fact that what you***

<u>are passing through at the moment is temporal. This too will pass away.</u>
Be it the chaos of war, the plague of an unexplainable pandemic, a failing marriage, or a disappointment in a relationship, a failed attempt in achieving your dream, the loss of a loved one, unending criticisms, name it. Please hold on to this, and to the fact that you are still alive for **a purpose**. Do not let depression steal that from you.

For every young person struggling with depression:

1) **Get your mind meaningfully engaged.**
   There are a lot of ways you can do this. Identify a healthy passion you have for any skill, and pursue it. It can be in any area. All it takes is identification. If a twelve-year-old can successfully bake, and decorate a cake, I don't think it should be so for anyone else.

Everything depends on your *creativity*.
All it takes is interest and determination. Depression

often comes from a feeling of low self-worth. It's a belief system that tells you that you are of no or little value, and have achieved nothing, or that your situation can never change. This is not true. You are special, you are unique, and you are you. There can't be another you. Keep your mind positively engaged. Depression can be persistent in approach. It does this when there are consistent criticisms, or there is a failure to achieve a goal you or others have set for you. If depressing thoughts become consistent, please talk to someone. Not just anyone, but a godly counselor who will help you out of your predicament.

In summary

You have life because **God** deemed it that it should be so. Every pain, disappointment, loss, trauma, or dissatisfaction has been ordained to either **make or mar** you.

Depression can be overcome. Put your heart to it. **Believe** that you can, and you will.

CHAPTER FOUR

Taking a glimpse at the picture of corporate slavery

Corporate slavery is a term that describes the unseen shackles hanging around the necks of employees in various establishments, due to harsh or degrading working conditions or environments.

Today, millions of graduates churned out by universities in various parts of the world, especially Africa, storm the labor market comprising public and private organizations for job opportunities. Employers understanding this trend have begun to exhibit an unspoken attitude that could be best described as "Exploitation". It is indeed a sad development, where for peanuts you are told that you are been 'helped'. Thousands of graduates chose to stay put with such situations, rather than staying idle, believing in a better tomorrow.

What are the effects of Corporate Slavery?

- Depression
- Emotional and psychological imbalance
- In extreme conditions, ill-health.
- Creates a feeling of low self-worth.
- May lead to nervous breakdowns if not properly checkmated on time.

How do you overcome Corporate Slavery?
The following are key elements to having freedom from corporate slavery:
• First, what do you want? Find out what you want, what you can tolerate, and what you can't. Set a target for yourself. Create

your niche, set your limits. Until you do that, you will keep been tossed to and fro by the waves of the corporate world. The story is told of a master's degree graduate in one of the African countries who got a teaching job in a basic school. Three months after the resumption of duty, she was informed one fateful day alongside her tutorial colleagues that they were not going to teach only, but that they would wash the toilets of their classes as well. What was the reason for this? Cleaners were in short supply. What would you have done if you were in her shoes? With no available job lurking nearby, and loads of responsibilities waiting to be catered for, the answer could be quite heavy to spill out. Yet, it gives a scary picture of what people pass through to make a living.

• Second, do you have the skills? It mustn't be something you knit or sew with your hands. It could be your acumen; is it business inclined, IT-driven, or as earlier mentioned, related to crafts? Find out what gives you joy and please work on them.

• Third, please stop believing that you must sit in a classroom or an office before money comes into your pocket. If you believe so, then it will keep working for you and against your growth as an individual.

• Fourth, pick with caution your company. Your company influences you, negatively or positively. Work with people who have giant ideas and concepts, tap into their wisdom, and get going with your dreams.

• Fifth, and most important, please do not give up. Sadly we live in a world that frowns at the word 'struggle', upholds cruelty, and sees it as an arsenal that ought to be possessed. Compassion and kindness are often seen as elements of weakness. Thus keep striving and don't give up, irrespective of your predicament. Don't forget the lifestyle of the ants. They work around the clock to ensure that their needs are met, no matter the hindrance or embargo in their way. While it is important to create a balance between work and rest, it would do us good if we pick some lessons from these tiny, yet wonderful creatures.

• Sixth, please if you are experiencing depression or any form of emotion outside joy or job satisfaction where you work, it means one thing; it's not the place for you. Please move on, and try to get something doing somewhere else. However, I am not ignorant of the fact that an alternative job may not be readily available. Thus if you are restricted because of this, you could do the following to avoid feeling suicidal.

- Develop what I call a thick skin to your working environment. These include the words and attitudes of your boss or colleagues. Let go of whatever is said or done towards you. In doing so, you set yourself free from every hurt. It's one thing to remember a hurt caused by someone. On the other hand, it is another thing to remain angry against your offenders.
- Work on your capabilities and develop yourself while you can. Attend seminars and workshops, read books, make new helpful friends, explore opportunities that come your way. Treat everyone around you with respect. You never can tell who may turn out to be your helper.

In conclusion, above every other thing, trust God and depend on HIM for all your needs.

CHAPTER FIVE

Addiction to certain vices

Emphasis will be laid on masturbation because it is the result of pornography.

Pornography is the display of nude persons engaged in various sexual activities.

Masturbation is the sexual stimulation of one's organs through one's thoughts or physical touch of one's private parts.

Alcoholism is the unrivaled commitment to drinking liquors until one loses his or her sense of reasoning.

The three all have one common effect; temporal loss of control over one's mind. Of the three, masturbation is more subtle.

The manifold effects of masturbation

According to goodnet.org, books provide plenty of mental stimulation, increases the activity in the brain's central sulcus, relaxes the brain, and temporarily transports itself to another world. From a study conducted at Emory University, reading puts you in someone else's shoes, through the brain's biology. It dawned on me, that you are mentally stimulated by what you read, negatively or positively. It's also interesting to note that reading puts you in someone else's shoes. So if you get engaged with a book that has erotic scenes, automatically, your mind replays it, with you as a mental participator. The same goes for what you view. As a human, your mind and your brain record what is displayed before it, and just like what reading does, the pictures exposed to your mind are automatically replayed by it. The chains that result from any addiction all began with what the mind was fed with. Masturbation begins from what you have exposed your mind to, either through wrong videos or reading the wrong books. Aside from this, it also:

- Creates room for other vices to come in.
- Undoubtedly creates a temporal loss of consciousness.
- Creates and accumulates trash in the individual's mind.
- Feeds an unnatural craving, and drive for sexual activities.
- For the Christian who understands the mystery and the connection between your mind, and what it is exposed to, it creates doorways for darker invasions.

In summary, here are the steps to overcoming masturbation:

1) Cut off **ALL** access to erotic, or sensually stimulating materials that often stimulate or provoke sensual thoughts.
2) Talk to a friend who is grounded in sound Christian principles or a friendly elder who is spiritually mature, about your challenges. These can help you, or help connect you to counseling and prayer.
3) As soon as you have access to the right counselor, please attend as many counseling sessions as you can. Talk about your struggles and challenges; be open, and receptive to every counsel received.
4) Please cultivate a relationship with God. Acknowledge that Jesus Christ is the only Lord and Savior you could ever have. Aside from your confessions to a counselor, confess your sins, and struggles in prayer, and hand them over to HIM. Pray consistently, try, and get a good Bible version, a daily devotional, and study the word of God **every day.** Pray with the promises you encounter each day in God's word, and learn to share

your progress with your counselor.

5)   Get your mind engaged positively. Take your thoughts away from sensual scenarios. Improve on your skills, and areas of interest. Always remember that you are special and that despite your many mistakes, God loves you, and will always be there for you, no matter what. All HE is waiting for is for you to come to HIM. HE is always waiting.

CHAPTER SIX

Now that you have overcome

You need to teach others what you were able to do to overcome your challenges. It mustn't be through a book, it could be done by sharing this orally, at a meeting, a dinner party, etc. Someone may need your experience.

Teaching is a skill on its own.

What is teaching?

In modern usage and to the common man, the words '**teaching**' and 'teacher' are wrapped up with schooling and schools.

One way of approaching the question is to look at what teachers do, and then draw out key qualities or activities that set them apart from others. The problem is that all sorts of things are bundled together in job descriptions or roles that may have little to do with what we can sensibly call teaching.

Another way is to head for the dictionaries and search for both the historical meanings of the term, and how it is used in everyday language. This brings us to definitions like;

- Impart knowledge to or instruct (someone) as to how to do something.
- Cause (someone) to learn or understand something **by example or experience**.

From these, we can say that **we are all teachers in some way at some time**, **be it as parents, superiors, supervisors, employers, employees, etc**.

Further insight is offered by looking at the ancestries of the word. For instance the origin of the word 'teach' lies in the Germanic originated word '*taecan*', meaning to show, present, or point out. This is simultaneously related to:

- The word '*token*', which has Indo-European roots.
- The Greek words '*deikunai*', (referring to the word 'show'), and '*deigma*', (referring to the word 'sample').

Why are we taking these theoretical tours? Paul Hirst (1975) concluded, that being clear about what teaching is, matters vitally because how teachers understand teaching, very much affects what they do in the classroom. The classroom here could be the actual hall dedicated to classes or a setting where knowledge is exchanged or passed across.

Teaching, therefore, is the process of attending to people's needs, experiences, feelings, and making specific interventions to help them learn particular things.

Interventions commonly take the forms of:

➢ Questioning
➢ Listening
➢ Giving information
➢ Explaining some phenomenon
➢ Demonstrating a skill or process.
➢ Testing the understanding and capacity of an individual.
➢ Learning activities.

CHAPTER SEVEN

The key elements of Teaching

✓　　Attending to people's feelings, experiences, and needs. Here, we consider:

　1)　The needs of those we are supposed to be teaching.

　2)　What might be going on for them?

✓　Focus.

Here, we should **be clear about what we are trying to do.** One of the findings that shine through research on teaching is that clear learning intentions help learners to see the point of a session or intervention, keep the process on track, and when challenging, make a difference in what people learn (Hattie 2009).

✓　**Subject Knowledge.**

Be it a lecture note, a sermon, a practical class, a presentation, a seminar, or an informal discussion between a parent and a child, teaching requires expertise and content. It has to involve both. Good teachers have deep knowledge of the subjects they teach, and when their knowledge level falls below this, it results in a significant impediment to the students learning.

✓　**Engaging people in learning.**

At the center of teaching lie enthusiasm, and a commitment to engage an individual in the learning process. This is how John Hattie (2009) puts it;

"It is teachers using particular teaching methods,

teachers with high expectations for all students, and teachers who have created positive student-teacher relationships that are more likely to have the above-average effects on student achievement."

CHAPTER EIGHT

Specific interventions involved in teaching.

· **Focusing on the different actions we take.**

Sometimes as teachers we fail to realize that our actions are often observed. It is when we see our actions replicated that it dawns on us. One morning, I had washed a set of clothes and was drying it, when I noticed that one of my kids was imitating what I had just done, by replaying the washing pattern I used. He held a piece of cloth and was washing it the way he had seen me doing it. Questioning, listening, explaining a phenomenon, demonstrating a skill or process, and facilitating learning activities are all part of the focus. But what is most is most important is to focus on the fact that our actions scream much louder than our words.

    ✓ **A conscious observation on how we shift between conversation moods.**
Conversations or discussions often experience shifts, such as a change in mood on the part of the teacher or learner.

    ✓ **Understanding that teaching is not a simple step-by-step process.**
This will help in instilling patience when it is demanded. Education includes the nurture of the child, and as it grows so also its culture. It is a complex process that depends on us to achieve the following:

    ✓ **Recognizing and cultivating teachable moments.**
This is very important in parent-child relationships.

    · Cultivating relationships in learning. This is attainable, even when large audiences of students are involved, as often seen in lecture hall settings in sub-Saharan Africa. While at the University, no matter how crowded the lecture hall was, there was this lecturer that always kept us spellbound. His name was Dr. Pam. He always introduced the lecture using jokes. He would then begin the lecture proper, and occasionally chip in stories. It was a common sight to see students holding their sides because they had laughed long and hard at his rib-cracking jokes. One fateful day, a female coursemate openly expressed her admiration for him. He widened his eyes and said without smiling;

"You asked late. After my wife has polished me through and through, and I am now a polished man, you are now coming to ask me out."

The whole class roared out in laughter.

When we had our final year dinner, he was the only one, the organizers felt free enough to approach, and invite. And he came, bearing that smile of his and that infectious disposition everyone wanted to experience.

- Accessing resources for learning. This could be retrieved from experience, expertise, interactions, etc.
- Adopting a growth mindset. Understanding that the person you are interacting with is also growing, in age, in the level of knowledge gained experience or expertise.

Some years back, I had the opportunity to teach a class of eighteen pupils. It was a mix-up of wards from the elite and middle-class families. But more importantly, they were separate individuals with different mindsets, upbringing, and orientations. You had the cool, calm, collected, and intelligent ones, like Treasure, and Shawn, who never reacted to any form of provocation from classmates, the insecure, such as Obinna who believed that when turned down by a classmate he admired, it was the end of the world. There were the domineering ones such as Munachi, who loved to get all the attention, and the loud ones such as Stephen, who never gave you a moment's rest.

One day, I found Munachi, sitting on a pile of textbooks to make her look taller. Was her aim, to gain attention? I would say yes. Because when I noticed what she was doing, she was looking away to see if any of her neighbors noticed what she had just done.

Stephen would never let you be, and he had a knack for doing the opposite of what he was asked to do. One day, I noticed during a math exercise that he was grossly occupied with something he was hiding in-between his books. I went to find out what was going on, and I found him looking at a comic book. The book was seized, and he was asked to do his classwork. The following morning, out of mere curiosity, I asked that he bring his school bag. My eyes nearly popped out. He not only forgot to bring his assignment but made sure he included all manner of toys and cartoon CDs. Honestly, I was at loss for words at that moment, because he stared back at me with these innocent eyes that said he did nothing wrong. I wondered then if the causative factor to his attitude was linked to the fact that he was the only male child out of seven children, or that his dad was a wealthy man, who was also a traditional ruler.

What is my point from all these? Then, these kids were all within a range of 7-9 years of age. If I were to meet them three years later, their reasoning, and attitude, won't be the same. But they will always remember the legacy you left for them.

This blend of characters and personalities is the same with our kids, our employees, colleagues at the office, superiors, etc.

Understanding that each person is unique in his or her way, **regardless** of age, profession, roots, or experience, is a key element we must all grasp in our daily routine of imparting knowledge, at home, at the office, in a lecture hall, on the pulpit, or elsewhere.

CHAPTER NINE

Teaching versus Indoctrination

Indoctrination involves knowingly encouraging people to believe regardless of the evidence. It also entails a lack of respect for their human rights.

Education, on the other hand, can be described as the wise, hopeful, and respectful cultivation of learning undertaken in the belief that all should have the chance to share in life.

The process of education flows from a basic orientation of respect, respect for truth, others, and themselves.

For teachers to be educators, they should:

- Take into account people's needs and wishes, now and in the future.
- Consider what might be good for all.
- Plan their interventions accordingly.

In conclusion,

Our world is the way it is today, because of the products of various forms of teaching. Wherever we find ourselves, at home, in the classroom or lecture hall, it is important to remember that at some point in our lives, we are teachers, like parents before our wards, as superiors before our employees, as colleagues in a working environment.

Teaching is not just a classroom technique. It goes beyond that.

When we fail to teach properly, we help in producing individuals who may be lacking in-home training, deficient in a skill or form of expertise, as well as a proper knowledge base. When we sight individuals sleeping during a sermon, lecture, or discussion, it is a simple indication that something is not right.

Understanding that it has to be done the right way, will go a long way in addressing a lot of errors in our society.

CHAPTER TEN

As parents...

Being a parent is one of the most amazing things you could ever experience if it is done right. You look back and you simply smile at the memories. But all these flows if we get it right. Parenting can be tricky, and lopsided. And until we find the appropriate balance, we may be found wanting at the end of the day. As I write this, I am also a student, learning from my mistakes, and sieving out the basic components I need to make things right. Are you ready for an eye-opening tour of tips you should bear in mind as a parent? Let's begin.

PARENTING TIPS

- ✓ As you stare at your newborn, bear it in mind that the child's mind is like a blank sheet, ready to be written on.
- ✓ Whether you believe it or not, your child watches you. And gleans his or her habits from what he or she has learned from you. It took me by storm when I found one of my wards chewing his fingers. I corrected him several times and wondered why he didn't stop until I found him staring at me as bit mine. I stopped midway as it dawned on me that he was doing what he had been doing because he had **seen me doing it.** I felt embarrassed, but the lesson stuck. No matter how irrelevant you think your actions are, your child is watching and eagerly learning.
- ✓ **Watch** your child and find out what he or she loves get-

ting engaged with, as they grow from weeks to months, and then to years. There is a purpose for which every individual is born. Children naturally exhibit what they are meant to be through what they often get engaged with. Find out what that is, and **encourage them to get improved in that field**. In some parts of the world, certain professions are considered superior to others. And because of this acclaimed 'superiority', some parents make the terrible mistake of **talking** their ward into studying what is trendy or popular, without taking into consideration what the child's passion is.

✓ **Teach the child healthy habits and lifestyles on time.** I had to learn this the hard way, especially with my first child. I failed to be firm with him at the onset. It took me time to realize that it was ungodly to do so. Children need a firm hand to guide them as they grow, and be churned out as the godly vessels they ought to be. If we as parents fail to realize that, no matter how much we try to dissociate ourselves from the actions of our babies when they eventually become adults, we will be held responsible for what we failed to do when we **should** have done it.

✓ **Learn to give your babies hugs.** No matter how little they are, they understand perfectly when a tender hug is shared, and reciprocate it subconsciously towards others. I never understood this, until I hugged a three-month-old baby. I almost cried when his little fingers grasped the neckline of my blouse. It was an amazing feeling as I watched this baby relax his head against my chest, his right hand on my shoulder, and his left holding on to the neckline of my blouse. When I wanted to lay him down in his cot, he refused to let go. I had to coax him to sleep before he did. Even babies desire to be loved, and we should do **all that we can as parents** to exhibit that love. It will go a long way in boosting their morale, and confidence as individuals. Nobler is the fact, that they will be individuals with a positive and healthy mental outlook on life. We live in a world that no longer regards integrity as a way of life. We need to instill that into our babies as they grow. They need to learn from us, from our actions that no matter what challenges they face, that no matter what they are been told, or what they pass through, that they are loved. This is important especially for our little girls. So many human predators have taken advantage of innocent, naïve girls because they were not grounded on these basic truths. Unfortunately, millions of such girls live with unforgettable scars gotten from unpleasant experiences.

✓ **Have or create time for your babies**. No matter how busy you are, create time for them. If you don't do so, someone else, or something else will. It won't be palatable if the influence exerted is a negative one. **Please** irrespective of your schedules, please create time for your babies and toddlers. Without your goodies, your presence goes a long way in molding the personalities of your babies.

✓ **Learn to observe and understand your child's temperament.** Observe what they like, and what they do not, find out what makes them sad, irritable, or happy. Be friends with your babies, encourage them to be honest with you, play with them when you have to. **Build their confidence and give them reasons why they should be free with you.** It all begins from the baby stages. You don't lock your child out as a baby and expect that child to grow close to you, or be honest or transparent with you as a pre-teen, or teenager. Do not leave everything about your child's welfare to someone else to handle on your behalf. A lot of adults today live secret lives and have become total strangers to their parents, because of this singular factor. They acted as one character under their parent's occasional watch, and as another when they are on their own.

✓ **Lead, teach by example.** Learn to curb unhealthy habits from your life, for the sake of your babies.
For parents who are Christians.

✓ **Teach your babies how to pray, by doing so before them**

daily.

✓ **Teach them basic truths. Introduce the word of God to them as soon as they can understand what you are saying. There are beautiful, well-illustrated bibles for children available at the appropriate outlets. Introduce these to your babies as they grow. Remember, that their minds and hearts are like a clean slate. It is what you expose them to, that is engrafted therein.**

✓ **Some have said that it doesn't matter but it does. Please mind what you expose your babies to. This is important, especially on TV.**

Finally

As a parent, we must understand the extreme relevance of these questions.

✓ What are my basic belief systems?

✓ What are my habits?

✓ What is my knowledge base, and personal faith founded on?

✓ Have I imparted this to my ward?

✓ Will, what I have imparted affect this child negatively or positively?

✓ Will this knowledge boost or reduce the confidence my child has?

✓ Will it help my child in the future?

CHAPTER ELEVEN

Remaining consistent in the path of Victory

To remain consistent in the path of victory, you have to be conversant with the infallible principles of prosperity. To remain victorious, you need to remain prosperous in whatever you chose to do. It could be a skill, a knowledge base, a way of life, etc.

The infallible principles of prosperity

INTRODUCTION

Prosperity is a popular word. Many however often misunderstand its true application to refer to only financial wealth. But it's more than that. Prosperity has a path that is unique to every individual. However, it is paved by principles that have to be observed. Take a tour as the infallible principles of prosperity are presented, and expounded on.

THE PATHWAYS TO ALL-ROUND PROSPERITY
DISCOVER YOUR PATH OF PROSPERITY AND OBEY ITS CALL.
- What are you living for?
- Have you come to understand your purpose in life?
- Are you still struggling to understand the directions you need to make headway in life?
- Are you satisfied with your achievements so far?
- Do you have any vision, any plan at all, on what you intend to achieve in life?

These are vital questions we must all answer. When they are successfully answered, then fifty percent of the hurdle has been crossed. If the answer to the set of questions above is a yes, then:

- Have I obeyed any specific burden, ideas, or concepts that have been tugging at my heart for a while now? Get this! If you have not yet obeyed that inner voice, that nagging idea in your head, that drumming concept that pops up before your eyes, day in, day out, you may be wandering away from your path of prosperity. The visions, ideas, and concepts sown in your spirit man are not just for the fun of it. They are your stepping stones to your prosperity.

If you have identified what you have passion for, have you taken any actions about that? It's one thing to have a dream; it's another to bring it to reality.

- Every mandate God has for humanity, needs a human vessel to accomplish it. Have you discovered what your divine mandate for humanity is? If you have not, please use this opportunity to discover what it is. If you have, then let's go to the next phase.

SUBMISSION TO SOURCES OF MENTORSHIP

- Every great man or woman had a mentor that helped him or she understands the rhetoric behind the path he or she is taking. The amazing thing about mentorship is that it could be obtained from:
  - A human who could use any of the following mediums listed below to pass across the required knowledge for mentorship.
  - An experience or chains of experiences.
  - A process or series of processes.
  - A material or materials, such as a book, an audio message, a video, etc.
  - A gathering such as a seminar, convention, workshop, etc.
- No one knows it all. For this fact, it is unwise to venture out on **your chosen path of prosperity** on your own, with no guidance whatsoever. Your convictions may be true, but you need some form of mentorship to **guide** you on that path.
- Understand that every genuine path of prosper-

ity never takes a day. Mentorship may take weeks, months, or years to obtain.

- Renew your **mentorship subscription as often as possible.** No matter how old you are in the field of your expertise, you need to renew your knowledge base. Your mind is the powerhouse of every path of prosperity ordained for you to tread on. It has to be renewed **consistently.**
- **Shed every aspect of your character that contradicts what you offer.** Great skills or productivity with a bad attitude produces a huge turnoff that causes huge setbacks.
- Every human ordained to be your mentor **must not be older than you.** It depends on how early you discover your path of prosperity. Thousands often wallow on the wrong paths, may experience financial abundance from it, but have no sense of achievement.

ESTABLISH YOUR CHANNELS OF VISIBILITY (For skills, business concepts, or corporate related performances).

You can do this by:

- Enhancing the knowledge obtained through mentorship. Churning out results that will speak for you wherever it goes. A well-made pair of sandals made in one geographical location can attract millions of interested buyers from all over the globe. All it takes is **expertise.** Outstanding ideas, presentations, field techniques, and solutions proffered for existing challenges, are evident outputs seen from individuals who work in the corporate realm.
- Creating awareness about your expertise. For corporate-inclined individuals, this is often exhibited through seminars and official presentations. For the craft-inclined individuals, uniqueness, quality, and durability are the watchwords for whatever you are creating awareness about.
- Being consistent with whatever you have presented, craft-wise or otherwise. If you began with a certain quality, maintain it. If you have been known for a certain level of productivity, maintain the tempo.

Lack of consistency sets you back on your quest for prosperity. I know of a certain matron who worked at a particular health center in the country. This lady was highly productive and exhibited this in the administration of every department of the clinic. Before long, women were trooping there in their numbers. A health center that was known for only immunization exercises soon began to offer antenatal and childbirth services. As though that was not enough, incentives such as free baby diapers were introduced during immunization exercises, the reception of the health center was equipped with a cable TV to keep waiting patients slightly occupied before been attended to, a borehole was drilled within the premises to ensure a consistent supply of water, etc. Two years later, this lady was posted to another area of the region, and someone else began to handle the health center. The difference between the two was screaming out. The previous matron was being sought out. Expectant, as well as nursing mothers, began to visit her home for consultations. As time went on, she had to set up a little booth beside her apartment to accommodate the visits. Women from far and near came to her. It seemed she had a touch of gold. Her productivity spoke for her, even when she was not there. So much did she impact on lives that she was given a jaw-dropping car model for a birthday gift. She was miles away from the metropolis, but it didn't stop women from coming to seek her counsel. She was prospering without going to the media houses to advertise what she was doing. Hundreds flocked to her weekly because of what she **consistently** offered humanity. Above all, when you speak with her, you are convinced that she is **happy and accomplished** with what she is doing. That is a true picture, and identity of prosperity.

- Expanding what you have successfully produced. This could be done by:

✓ Including services related to your expertise that solves a particular challenge. Let's take the case study of the matron. She was given a health center to supervise. In her wisdom, she included antenatal and childbirth services. A borehole was drilled, addressing the challenge of water shortages, and so on.

✓ Improving the existing quality of the product already presented to the populace.

✓ Creating avenues for feedback.

✓ Setting aside seasons for incentives, freebies, appreciations, inclusion of hamper packages in your products, name it, the list is endless.

✓ Applying creativity in what you already offer. Are you a craft-inclined individual? Include delivery services in your existing offers, gifts in your delivery parcels or bags, etc. It all depends on your creativity, financial strength, customer base, and demand.

In conclusion

Prosperity has laid down principles that cannot be skipped. To gain access to prosperity, we need to:

- **Identify what our divine mandate in life is, and obey its call.**
- **Submit ourselves to sources of mentorship.**
- **Establish our channels of visibility.**
- **Improve on the quality of whatever we offer to humanity.**
- **Expand on existing ideas, concepts, products, or services.**
- **Consistently renew our minds, and shed off undesirable behavior.**

IN SUMMARY

The key to overcoming challenges that hinder your productivity lies in a combination of decisions and actions that improves the output of whatever you do.

- Identify the negativity.
- Undertake the steps to overcome it.
- Be consistent in the path of the victory you have obtained.
- If you are a parent, you need to review your role in parenting.
- Get conversant with the infallible principles of prosperity.

ABOUT THE AUTHOR

Christy Obidigwe

An author, writer, and mother, who loves to reach out to others using her writings. Helping others overcome their challenges, gives her joy. Any correspondence can be made to her blog (https://www.alwaysgivinghope.blogspot.com).

BOOKS BY THIS AUTHOR

The Visions Of A Seer

The adventures of a young woman who has a very rare gift.

www.ingramcontent.com/pod-product-compliance
Lightning Source LLC
Chambersburg PA
CBHW060920130726
48001CB00006B/2332